EXTREME ANIMALS

VAMPIRE

BATS

To Chloe and Ruby

Who think there is something fascinating about vampires in twilight.

Acknowledgments

Special thanks to my superb editor, Jenne Abramowitz. Thanks also to Kevin Callahan
for his excellent design and to Elizabeth Van Houten for her skillful copyediting.
The author is grateful to David Reuther for his editorial and design suggestions,
as well as his enthusiasm for this project.

Photo Credits

Front cover: © Barry Mansell/naturepl.com; back cover and page 5: © Tom McHugh/
Photo Researchers, Inc.; pages 1 and 32: © Michael Lynch/Shutterstock;
pages 3 and 18–19: © Adrian Warren/Ardea; pages 6–7, 13, 16 (bottom), and 17 (top):
© Dr. Merlin D. Tuttle/Bat Conservation International/Photo Researchers, Inc.; page 6 (bottom): © Michael
Lynch/Almay; page 7 (top): © James H. Robinson/Photo Researchers, Inc.; pages 7 (bottom) and 22–23:
© Stephen Dalton/Photo Researchers, Inc.; pages 8, 16 (top), and 17 (bottom): © Dr. Merlin D. Tuttle/Photo
Researchers, Inc.; page 9: © Stephen J. Krasemann/Photo Researchers, Inc.; pages 10–11: © Eric and David
Hosking/Corbis; pages 14–15: © B. G. Thomson/Photo Researchers, Inc.; page 15: © Untitled X-Ray/Nick
Veasey/Getty Images; page 21: © Bruce Dale/National Geographic/Getty Images; page 24–25:
© Carsten Peter/Getty Images; pages 26–27: © Zigmund Leszczynski/Animals Animals; pages 28–29:
© Jake Schoellkopf/AP Photo; page 30: © Michael C. Gray/Shutterstock; page 31: © Associated Press.

ISBN-13: 978-0-545-16193-0
ISBN-10: 0-545-16193-2

12 11 10 9 8 7 6 5 4 3 2 1   9 10 11 12 13 14/0

Printed in the U.S.A.
First printing, October 2009

EXTREME ANIMALS

VAMPIRE BATS

Seymour Simon

scholastic inc.

New York   Toronto   London   Auckland
Sydney   Mexico City   New Delhi   Hong Kong

Vampires are real. Vampire bats, that is. These mysterious mammals travel in the shadows of the night, hunting for food before returning to their darkened caves. But how much do you really know about vampire bats? Do you think that they have fangs or suck blood? And where do vampire stories come from? In this book, you'll find out the fact and fiction about vampire bats.

Vampire bats are real.

As evening falls, vampire bats fly out of caves, tree hollows, abandoned buildings, and barns. They wing through the night air in search of food, almost invisible in the darkness. And like legends of the vampires from which they get their name, vampire bats feed on blood. But vampire bats only rarely bite people.

Unlike many other bats, which only fly, vampire bats can walk, run, and jump. They have strong hind legs that help launch their bodies into the air.

There are three species of vampire bats: white-winged, hairy-legged, and common.

white-winged
vampire bat

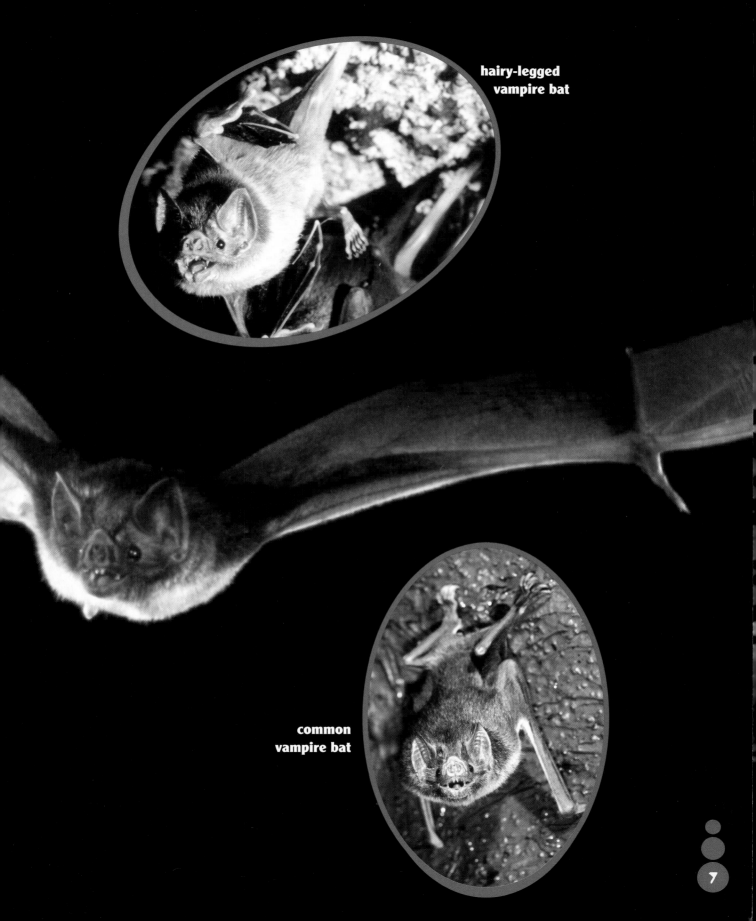

hairy-legged
vampire bat

common
vampire bat

7

Bats are helpful to people.

F A C T

There are around 1,000 different kinds of bats. Most bats eat insects, which helps control the insect population. One small brown bat can catch 600 flying insects per hour. Some bats eat insects that feed on crops. That means people can use fewer chemicals and poisons to protect food crops. Other bats help pollinate flowers and spread seeds. Vampire bats might be helpful, too. Scientists are studying their saliva. They think the saliva might help them discover new blood and heart medications.

Mexican free-tailed bats live in caves in Texas and New Mexico. A colony of Mexican free-tailed bats can eat more than a dozen tons of insects in a single night. That's more than 24,000 pounds of bugs!

vampire bats are huge.

FICTION

Vampire bats are small and lightweight. Their body is less than three inches long. That's about the size of your thumb. They have an eight-inch wingspan, which would barely cover the width of a sheet of notebook paper. They only weigh as much as five nickels. Vampire bats are so light that they can drink blood from a sleeping animal without waking it up.

BIG AND TALL vs ITTY BITTY

Some bats are even smaller than vampire bats. The Philippine bamboo bat weighs only 1/20 of an ounce, less than the weight of one dime. The largest bats are the "flying foxes" of Africa and Asia. They can weigh more than two pounds and have a six-foot wingspan.

Vampire bats live in warm climates.

F A C T

All three kinds of vampire bats live in the warm climates of Mexico, Central America, and the northern parts of South America. Vampire bats can be found along the equator living at sea level and in the mountains. As temperatures warm worldwide, vampire bats might someday migrate north and begin to live in southern Florida and Texas.

RED, WHITE, AND BAT

There are about 50 kinds of bats that live in the United States. They live in every state—including Hawaii and the southern parts of Alaska.

Bats are birds.

F I C T I O N

Bats have wings, but they are not birds. Bats do not have feathers. They don't build nests or lay eggs. Bats are mammals. Their bodies are covered with hair. Bats are born live—they don't hatch from eggs. They drink their mother's milk when they are babies.

Bats are the only mammals that can really fly. Some mammals, like flying squirrels, can glide through the air for long distances. But bats fly in many different ways. Some bats hover in midair. Other bats dart and twist through the night skies as they catch insects. Larger bats soar high above the ground.

WEIRD WINGS

Bat wings are like human hands, except they have a thin membrane of skin between each "finger bone." Bats move their wings like hands, "swimming" through the air.

F I C T I O N

Vampire bats are the only kind of bat that feeds on blood. Most bats eat fruit or flowers. About 700 kinds of bats eat insects. A few bats, like the false vampire bat of Southern Mexico and Central America, eat animals.

The fisherman bat feeds on small fish. It circles near the water and catches them with its large, sharp, curved claws. These bats can swim well. They use their wings as oars.

The false vampire bat eats birds, small land animals such as mice, snakes, and reptiles, and even smaller bats. This bat is the largest meat-eating bat in the world. It has a wingspan of almost three feet.

Vampire bats feed on animal blood.

F A C T

Vampire bats feed on blood from chickens, cows, pigs, and horses. They have also been known to feed on human blood, although those cases are rare.

Vampire bats are very small. They only eat about one tablespoon of blood in a night. Sometimes several vampire bats will feed on an animal at the same time. Usually, their prey doesn't wake up or notice that it has been bitten. But if the animal is small or sick, it may die from the loss of blood. Vampire bats may carry diseases such as rabies that they can pass to their prey.

NIGHT BITES

Vampire bats hunt in the darkness of the night. Their prey is usually asleep and easy to approach. And that's when vampire bats are least likely to be caught by other nighttime predators, such as owls.

Vampire bats suck blood through their fangs.

Vampire bats do not suck blood.
They lap it up. First, the bat carefully licks the skin of its prey to soften it and flatten down any hairs that are in the way. Then the bat holds a tiny fold of its prey's skin in its mouth. It takes a short jump backward while biting with its razor-sharp front teeth. A vampire bat's front teeth are so sharp that its bite is almost painless.

The bite is tiny, but deep. The animal begins to bleed freely. A chemical in the bat's saliva prevents blood clotting so that blood continues to flow while the bat laps it up. If the bat is not disturbed, feeding usually lasts about 20 minutes.

BLOODIVORE

A vampire bat's only source of food is blood. The bat's throat is too narrow to swallow solid food.

Bats are blind.

All bats can see. Some have bad eyesight, while others see better than humans. But bats use their ears rather than their eyes to navigate and hunt for night-flying insects. They squeak in short bursts of high-pitched sounds. The sounds bounce off insects and objects in the bat's path.

Bats fly back and forth in the night sky in odd patterns. But they aren't just having fun. They are chasing small, flitting insects.

Then they echo back to the bat's ears. The bat can determine the distance and direction of the echoes. This is called echolocation. Echolocation is also used by dolphins and some other animals.

Vampire bats live in colonies.

F A C T

Vampire bats live in groups called colonies. Colonies of vampire bats can range from just a few bats to thousands. They often roost with other kinds of bats. A small colony of vampire bats usually has one adult male bat with a dozen or more females and their young.

Vampires usually fly in groups of two to six. When the bats return to their colony, they often meet and groom one another. A bat that has been successful on the hunt may offer blood to an unsuccessful colony mate. Vampire bats cannot survive two nights in a row without a meal. Sharing blood helps the colony survive.

FAST FOOD

Vampire bats usually return to their roosts in caves, hollow trees, and abandoned buildings within two hours of setting out. They spend the rest of the night digesting their meal.

vampire bats strike from the air.

A vampire bat doesn't strike from the air like a hawk dive-bombing its prey. The bat circles around a sleeping animal for several minutes. Then it lands on the animal or on the ground next to it.

Vampire bats creep toward sensitive areas of their prey like the neck, back, or underbelly. Sometimes three or four vampire bats feed on the same animal.

SPEED DEMONS

Vampire bats are great runners and hoppers. They can run at speeds of nearly five miles per hour.

Baby vampire bats drink milk.

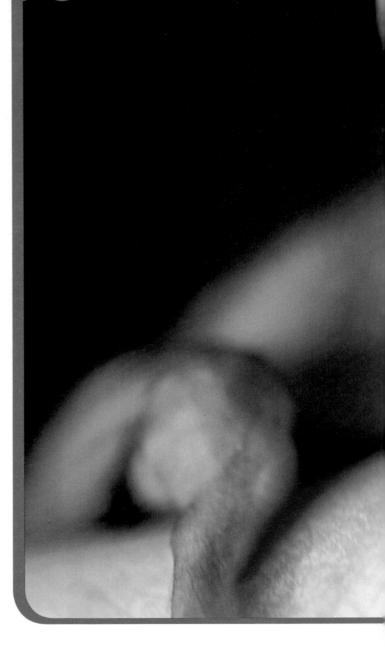

A mother vampire bat usually gives birth to one baby at a time. A baby vampire bat is born without hair. Its tiny wings are pink and weak. The mother nurses its baby with a mixture of milk and blood.

The mother carries the baby with her when she hunts. Eventually the baby gets too large to carry, and she must leave it behind in the colony. But she'll find it again easily. Each baby has a unique scent that its mother recognizes.

Baby vampire bats learn to fly in three or four months. Then they can join their mothers on hunting trips.

The legend of Dracula is based on vampire bats.

FICTION

Many people believe that the story of Dracula and myths about human vampires developed out of the study of vampire bats. But the truth is that vampire bats got their name from  stories about human vampires, not the other way around.

In European myths and stories, vampires are people who have returned from the dead to feed upon the blood of living people.

When European explorers came to the New World and found blood-feeding bats, they gave them the name "vampires."

Of course these bats were well-known to the people of South and Central America. The bats had many other names before they were discovered by Europeans.

SCARY STORY

Bram Stoker read stories about bats that fed on blood. He incorporated these bat facts into his book *Dracula*.

The world portrays bats as scary animals of the dark because they are linked to vampire myths. But now you know the real facts. Vampire bats are simply flying mammals who hunt for food. And like all predators, vampire bats are fierce, fascinating creatures of nature.